I Am the Cat

I Am the Cat

by Alice Schertle • illustrated by Mark Buehner

Lothrop, Lee & Shepard Books • New York

In the alley, a
stray cat drinks the round white moon
from a rain puddle

The Cat's Version

In the beginning,
when the Cat could fly,
the Master placed a pan
of white milk
in the sky.
"The world is yours,"
he told the Cat.
"Eat everything. Grow fat.
Live off the land.
Keep only this command:
You must not drink the moon."

And so the Cat was mistress
of both earth and sky.
(I told you that
the Cat
could fly.)
She soared on silken wings
as owl or kestrel might,
and dropped with ease
to seize
whatever pleased her appetite.

But, oh! The moon!
Her green eyes burned
to see it hanging there.
And when her Master's
back was turned,
she flew up through the air
and drank it dry.
Then, seeing what she did,
she sank down
from the sky
and hid.

She licked her paw
and rubbed her face.
She could not wash away
the trace of sin.
The Master found the Cat
with moonmilk
on her chin.
His awful voice cried,
"Scat!"
And so she fell from grace.
He took away
her wings....

You understand,
the Cat
has had a taste
of higher things
than living low like
common bugs and frogs,
keeping alleyways,
and being chased
by dogs.

My cat strolls into
the house with one small feather
stuck to her whisker

I Am the Cat

I am the cat in the easy chair—
    velvet arms, and a cushion where
I scratch my claws and groom my hair—
    Mine, alone, is the easy chair.

I am the cat in a puddle of sun—
    isn't a sun puddle wonderful fun?
Doesn't the light make my dark coat shine?
    Isn't it right that the sun is mine?

I am the cat in the wild, wild weeds
    watching a thing with eyes like seeds,
ears like petals on a small pink rose,
    sliver of tail, quiver of nose,

bones and blood and delicate feet—
    doesn't a warm gray mouse smell sweet?
Little heart beating, skull and spine—
    Mine!

Paw by paw she steps
delicately onto the
book I am reading

Sophie, Who Taunted the Dogs

Sophie the Cat
took peculiar delight
in taunting
the neighborhood dogs every night.

On top of a wall
she reclined like a queen,
too high to be reached . . .
but easily seen.

Cockers and collies
assembled beneath her.
They leaped and they lunged—
but they couldn't quite reach her.

She relished their anguish.
(She loved being bad.)
"Meow," she said softly.
(The sound drove them mad.)

Languidly posing,
she watched the dogs pace.
With one silken paw
she'd be washing her face.

She wouldn't come closer—
too clever for that.
Outrageous.
Courageous.
Incredible cat!

When the mongrels assembled
one ill-fated night,
she looked down from her wall
and observed
with delight

a new dog among them—
a shaggy recruit
with great slavering jaws.
Sophie yawned at the brute.

She half closed her eyes;
she started to purr;
with exquisite boredom she
taunted
the cur.

Then, arching her back
with magnificent grace,
she showed him her teeth—
and she spat in his face.

His legs tensed beneath him
like tightly coiled springs . . .
He shot through the air
like a creature with wings!

Like a hound come from hell—
brimstone in his wake—
the mongrel could jump!
Sophie saw her mistake.

She was faster than lightning,
but not fast
enough.
From the mouth of the fiend
came a bloodcurdling
"Wuff!"

The last thing she heard
was a triumphant growl
as his jaws closed around her.

'Twas murder most foul.

A moment of silence.
A moment of prayer.
For all that is left
is a tooth and a hair
of a feline phenomenon:
Sophie Sublime,
who has taunted the dogs
for the very
last
time.

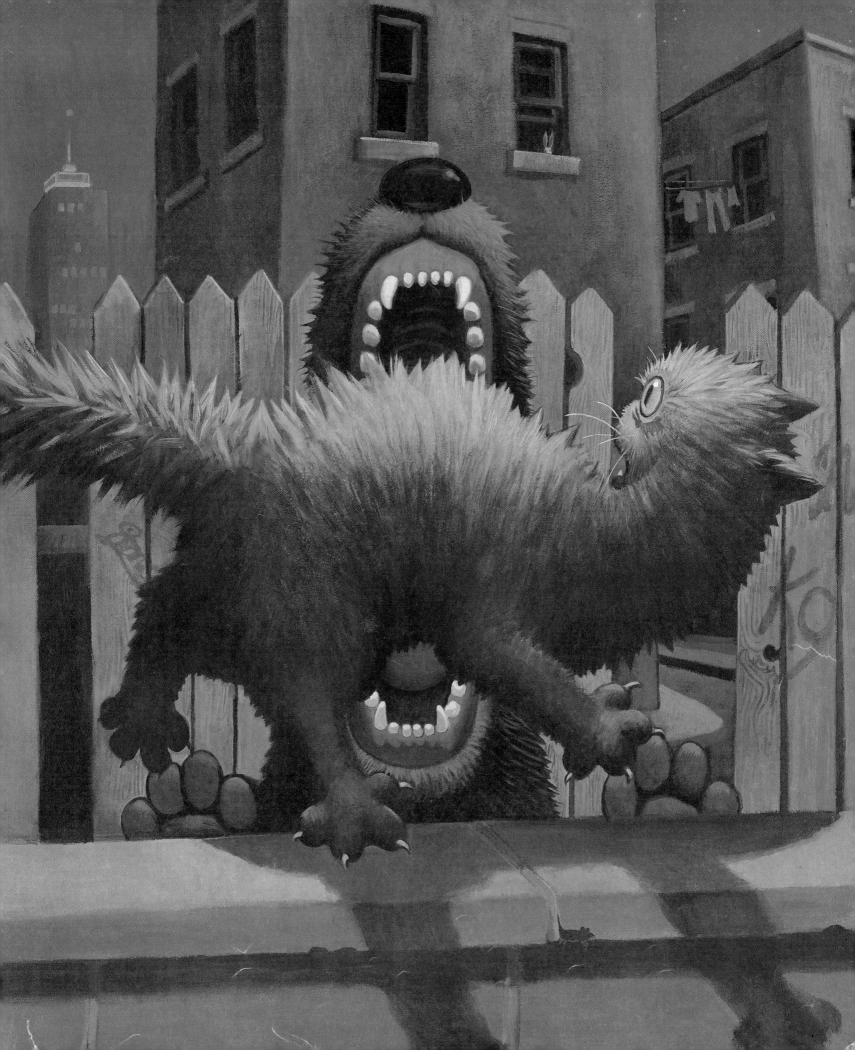

And still, it is said, when the moon rises round
and gold as a cat's eye, the dogs hear a sound . . .

Is it only the rustle of wind through the trees?
No dog among them can trust what he sees.

That devilish voice—
        how it hunts them and haunts them!
That soft, silken song—
        how it teases and taunts them!

They snap at the shadows and hear, even now,
        a magical,
                musical,
                        mellow
                            "Meow!"

She flows around my
ankles, lapping in soft gray
waves against my legs

To a Kitten

You stalk a string, subdue a flannel mouse,
     on hunter's paws prowl through my house
alert for balls of dust and other prey.

A raindrop sliding down the windowpane
     will make you wild. You entertain
us both with your assaults upon the glass.

Creep toward my finger—leap! And when you land,
     I'll hold you purring in my hand
to feel beneath your ribs a tiger's heart.

Wrapped in the perfect
curve of her tail, she poses
motionless as stone

One velvet funnel
swivels, scooping up the thin
twitterings of birds

Her amber eyes tell
me that temples were built . . . once . . .
to honor the cat

for Susan Pearson

AS & MB

Acrylic and oil paints were used for the full-color illustrations.
The text type is 20-point Della Robbia.
Design by David Neuhaus.

Text copyright © 1999 by Alice Schertle
Illustrations copyright © 1999 by Mark Buehner

Published by Lothrop, Lee & Shepard Books
a division of William Morrow and Company, Inc.
1350 Avenue of the Americas, New York, NY 10019
www.williammorrow.com

Printed in the United States of America.

10 9 8 7 6 5 4 3 2 1

Library of Congress Cataloging-in-Publication Data
Schertle, Alice.
I am the cat/by Alice Schertle; illustrated by Mark Buehner.
p. cm.
Summary: A series of poems about cats.
ISBN 0-688-13153-0 (trade)—ISBN 0-688-13154-9 (library)
1. Children's poetry, American. 2. Cats—Juvenile poetry. [1. Cats—Poetry. 2. American poetry.]
I. Buehner, Mark, ill. II. Title. PS3569.C48435I18 1999 811'.54—dc21 98-21306 CIP AC